D0032809

PARADIGMS

The Business of
Discovering the Future

Joel Arthur Barker

HarperBusiness
A Division of HarperCollins*Publishers*

A hardcover edition of this book was published in 1992 under the title *Future Edge* by William Morrow and Company, Inc. It is here reprinted by arrangement with William Morrow and Company, Inc.

PARADIGMS. Copyright © 1992 by Joel Arthur Barker. All rights reserved. Printed in the United States of America. No part of this book may be used or reproduced in any manner whatsoever without written permission except in the case of brief quotations embodied in critical articles and reviews. For information address HarperCollins Publishers, Inc., 10 East 53rd Street, New York, NY 10022.

HarperCollins books may be purchased for educational, business, or sales promotional use. For information please write: Special Markets Department, HarperCollins Publishers, Inc., 10 East 53rd Street, New York, NY 10022.

First HarperBusiness edition published 1993.

Designed by Lynn Dorofino Designs

Library of Congress Cataloging-in-Publication Data

Barker, Joel Arthur.
    [Future edge]
    Paradigms : the business of discovering the future / Joel Arthur Barker. — 1st ed.
      p.   cm.
    Originally published: Future edge. 1st ed. New York : W. Morrow, c1992.
    Includes bibliographical references and index.
    ISBN 0-88730-647-0 (pbk.)
    1. Business forecasting. 2. Forecasting. 3. Paradigms (Social sciences)
    4. Success in business. I. Title.
    [HD30.27.B36   1993]
    658.4'0355—dc20   92-54950

97 RRD   20 19

To my mother and father who were never both-
ered by my being a little weird

And to my son, Andrew, who was and still is my
greatest teacher

And to my wife, Susan, who has stuck
with me through thick and thin and
has been and still is my partner in
business and life

Acknowledgments

WHILE THE WRITING of a book is a solitary activity, the experiences and help that prepared me came from many people over the past two decades. I would like to thank, in particular, those people who helped me at the crucial times in my development as a futurist and author.

Thanks to **Tom Read** for giving me permission to leave my teaching position at St. Paul Academy and Summit School to explore what the futures studies movement was all about; to **David Lilly** for providing the funds for that fellowship; to **Dennis Meadows,** childhood friend, who gave me a chance to study the questions of Limits to Growth with his team in Copenhagen; to Professor **James Bright,** who became my first mentor in the field of futures studies; to **T. Lance Holthusen,** who brought me into the Science Museum of Minnesota and then promoted me into his own job as director of the Futures Studies Department because he thought I could do a better job; to my wife, **Susan,** for encouraging me to take the leap and become an independent consultant and lecturer; to **Bill Weimer,** mentor and friend, who was first to recognize the deep importance of the paradigm discussion for corporations and gave me my first contact with IBM; to **Scott Erickson,** my friend and partner, who always challenged me to

7

improve my work on paradigms; to **Ray Christensen,** who had the courage to partner with me in the making of my video *Discovering the Future: The Business of Paradigms;* to **Jaymie Mitchell,** who helped me with the graphic preparation of my manuscript; to **Margret McBride,** my wonderful agent, who brought me to William Morrow and my most excellent editor, **Adrian Zackheim.**

Contents

Foreword

FOR THE PAST FOUR YEARS I have been describing three keys to the future for any organization, profit or nonprofit, that wants to participate fully in the twenty-first century.

They are:

Anticipation

Innovation

Excellence

When I ask my audiences if they agree with the importance of three "keys," they always do. It is hard to argue with them. And yet many organizations think one or two of the three are enough.

All three are necessary.

Let me tell you why.

11

Excellence is at the base of the list because it is the base of the twenty-first century. Many in my audiences justify the importance of excellence (or Total Quality Management, as it is also called) because they believe it will give them a competitive edge in the twenty-first century. I don't believe that. I say it will give them a competitive edge only until the end of the decade. After that, it becomes the necessary price of entry.

If you do not have the components of excellence—statistic process control, continuous improvement, benchmarking, the constant pursuit of excellence, the capability of knowing how to do the right thing the first time (all of these derive from the same philosophy created by W. Edwards Deming and O. M. Juran and universalized by them and people like Philip Crosby)—then **you don't even get to play the game.**

Innovation is on the list because it **is** the way you gain competitive edge. Innovation coupled with excellence—which the Japanese have done so well—is a powerful combination. In the twenty-first century, no one will always be the leader. The top four or five positions within an industry will change frequently. But it is in the top four or five positions that you want to be. Lower than that will require you to price your copycat products at a commodity level, and that will leave you with insufficient margin to pay for the research and development necessary to work your way up to the top level.

However, excellence and innovation are not enough.

Anticipation provides you with the information that allows you to be in the right place at the right time with your excellent innovative product or service.

Too many times we have seen great ideas arrive too late: the Univac personal computer, Federal Express Zap mail. And we have also seen great ideas arrive too early: AT&T Picturephone; Apple's Macintosh (lucky for Steve Jobs that Steve Wozniak stuck to the knitting with the Apple II, which allowed the Macintosh to wait for its right time—desktop publishing time).

Anticipation is the final element of the triad. This triad allows you to predict your customer needs, innovate the products or services required to fulfill them, and produce those products and services excellently. With these three attributes you are ready not just to survive in the twenty-first century but to thrive!

This book is about innovation and anticipation. It will make you better at both.

CHAPTER 1

Watching for the Future

The future is where our greatest leverage is.

LET ME share with you a true story that began in 1968. It illustrates why we need to learn how to explore the future.

In 1968, if anyone had been asked the following question, you would have expected the same answer: In 1990 what nation will dominate the world of watchmaking?

The answer—Switzerland.

Why? Because Switzerland had dominated the world of watchmaking for the past sixty years. The Swiss made the best watches in the world. Anyone who wanted a good watch, an accurate watch, bought a Swiss watch.

And the Swiss were constantly improving their watches. They had invented the minute hand and the second hand. They led the research in discovering better ways to manufacture the gears, the bearings, and the mainsprings of modern watches. They were on the cutting edge of research in waterproofing watches. They brought to market the best self-winding watches. They were constant innovators.

What I am trying to point out is that the Swiss didn't just rest on their laurels. They continually worked at making better watches.

By 1968 they had done so well that they had more than 65 percent of the unit sales in the world watch market and more than 80 percent of the profits (some experts estimated as high as 90 percent). They were the world leaders in watchmaking by an enormous stretch. No one was even a close second.

Yet by 1980 their market share had collapsed from 65 percent to less than 10 percent. Their huge profit domination had dropped to less than 20 percent. By all significant measures, they had been ignominiously dethroned as the world market leader.

What happened?

Something profound.

They had run into a **paradigm shift**—a change in the fundamental rules of watchmaking. The mechanical mechanism was about to give way to electronics. Everything the Swiss were good at—the making of gears and bearings and mainsprings—was irrelevant to the new way.

And so, in less than ten years, the Swiss watchmaking future, which had seemed so secure, so profitable, so dominant, was destroyed. Between 1979 and 1981, fifty thousand of the sixty-two thousand watchmakers lost their jobs. And, in a nation as small as Switzerland, it was a catastrophe.

For another nation, however, it was the opportunity of a lifetime. Japan, which had less than 1 percent of the world watch market in 1968 (even though their mechanical watches were almost as good as those of the Swiss), was in the midst of developing world-class electronic technology. The electronic quartz watch was a natural derivative. Seiko led the charge, and today the Japanese have about 33 percent of the market, with an equivalent share of the profits.

The irony of this story for the Swiss is that the situation was totally avoidable if only the Swiss watch manufacturers had known how to think about their own future. If only they had known the kind of change they were facing: a paradigm shift.

Because it was the Swiss themselves who invented the electronic quartz movement at their research institute in Neuchâtel, Switzerland. Yet, when the Swiss researchers presented this revolutionary new idea to the Swiss manufacturers in 1967, it was rejected.

After all, it didn't have a mainspring, it didn't need bearings, it required almost no gears, it was battery-powered, it was electronic. **It couldn't possibly be the watch of the future.** So sure were the manufacturers of that conclusion that they let their researchers showcase their useless invention at the World Watch Congress that year. Seiko took one look, and the rest is history.

How can you avoid the mistake the Swiss made? And, keep in mind, the Swiss watch industry isn't the only one that has made such a mistake. Nations have done it. Many corporations and organizations have done it. Individuals have done it. We are all susceptible.

My task is to help you avoid the Swiss mistake by improving your ability to anticipate the future.

Most people know the future only as a place that is always robbing them of their security, breaking promises, changing the rules on them, causing all sorts of troubles. And yet, **it is in the future where our greatest leverage is.** We can't change the past, although if we are smart, we learn from it. Things happen only in one place—the present. And usually we react to those events. The "space" of time in the present is too slim to allow for much more. It is in the yet-to-be, the future, and only there, where we have the time to prepare for the present.

If we can learn to anticipate the future better, we need not fear it. In fact, we can welcome it, embrace it, prepare for its coming, because more of it will be the direct outgrowth of our own efforts.

We may not be able to discern the exact size of the future, but we can surely do better, through exploration, in obtaining significant data about its probable outline and direction. In fact, we need to if we want to begin to shape our own future. We are going to focus on a single concept that can help us do a much better job of anticipating the future. And while we learn to anticipate, we will also learn how to be more innovative through both discovery and creation.

Why is that intelligent people with good motives do such a poor job at anticipating the future?

We are going to examine several of the key principles that explain this apparent contradiction. These principles are embedded in a discussion of paradigms and how they change. These principles not only explain why people do not anticipate the future well; they explain how to improve your ability to see aspects of the future that may otherwise be totally invisible to you. And I promise you, because I have seen it repeatedly, that by understanding the Paradigm Principles you will be able to open doorways to your future that would have otherwise stayed locked up until it was too late. Just like the Swiss.

As more than one sage has already observed, the future is where you are going to spend the rest of your life. And since that is true, wouldn't it be useful to be able to get to know more about the neighborhood before you move in?

CHAPTER 2

The Importance of Anticipation

You can and should shape your own future. Because, if you don't, someone else surely will.

THE FIELD OF FUTURE STUDIES became familiar to the public when Alvin Toffler published his now classic *Future Shock* in 1970. That book demonstrated to a wide audience the importance of trying to anticipate the future, to understand potential long-term implications of change, both positive and negative, before they occurred.

Future studies, or futurism or futurology, already had a substantial although secluded life long before Toffler appeared on the scene. Study of the future began during World War II in the military and was continued after the war by the RAND Corporation, Stanford Research Institute (now SRI International), Ted Gordon's Futures Group, and the Hudson Institute. The concept of studying the future grew in a serious and rigorous way throughout the 1950s and 1960s.

But it took the social and political chaos and resulting turbulence of the 1970s to bring this field of study out of the scholarly closet and into the living room of public visibility. These days we expect to read articles about the future in popular magazines, to find books about the future in our local bookstore, and to watch TV shows whose primary purpose is to give us information about possible futures ahead. The study of the future is a part of our conceptual landscape because we, as members of a global society, have come to value the skills of anticipation.

The field of future studies can be broken up into two general areas: **content futurism** and **process futurism**. A content futurist is a person who specializes in an area of information about the future. Whether it is robotics or telecommunications, energy or water usage, shelter design or nutrition, content futurists speculate on the "whats" of the future. Process futurism, the area I have chosen to focus on, deals with **how** to think about the "whats." In my own work, I have often found that people have significant amounts of content about possible futures but have no way of making that information useful. Process futurists teach them how to manipulate that information.

I want to teach you about a concept that can help you to discover the future with greater accuracy. It is a way of fishing for the future.

In the last twenty years, all of Western society has passed through extraordinarily turbulent times. We have been living in a time when fundamental rules, the basic ways we do things, have been altered dramatically. That is, what was right and appropriate in the early 1960s is now, in many cases, wrong and highly inappropriate in the 1990s. Or, conversely, what was impossible, crazy, or clearly out of line in the early 1960s is, in many cases today, so ordinary that we forget that it wasn't always that way. These dramatic changes are extremely important because they have created in us a special sense of impermanence that generates tremendous discomfort.

Let's take a look at an abbreviated list of these fundamental changes in technology and society:

- The introduction of environmentalism (everything living is interconnected; there is no such thing as a free lunch) as a legitimate way of perceiving the world.

- Terrorism as an everyday activity.

- Rampant inflation in the United States during the 1970s and 1980s.

- Deregulation of banking, the airlines, the telecommunications and trucking industries.

- The loss of the United States's position as the leading-edge manufacturer of the world (for example, of VCRs).

- VCRs.

- Civil rights.

- The growth of participatory management in the United States.

- The loss of respect for major institutions such as the Supreme Court, the police, the federal government, the Congress.

- The almost total disappearance of union power.

- The emergence of information as a key resource.